Body Power

Contents **Page**

written by Samantha Montgomerie

Red Rocket Readers™
Engineered by Flying Start Books

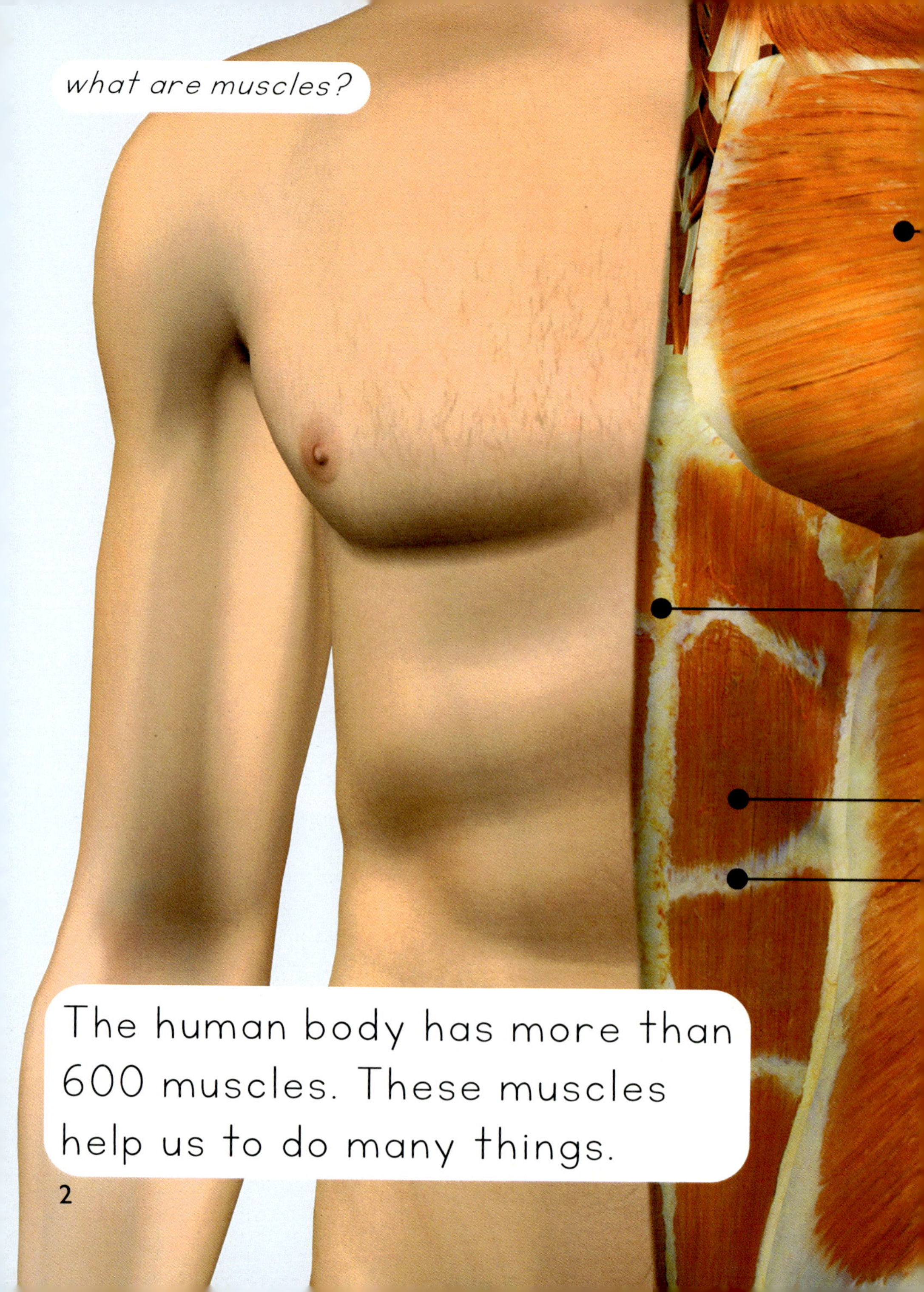

The human body has more than 600 muscles. These muscles help us to do many things.

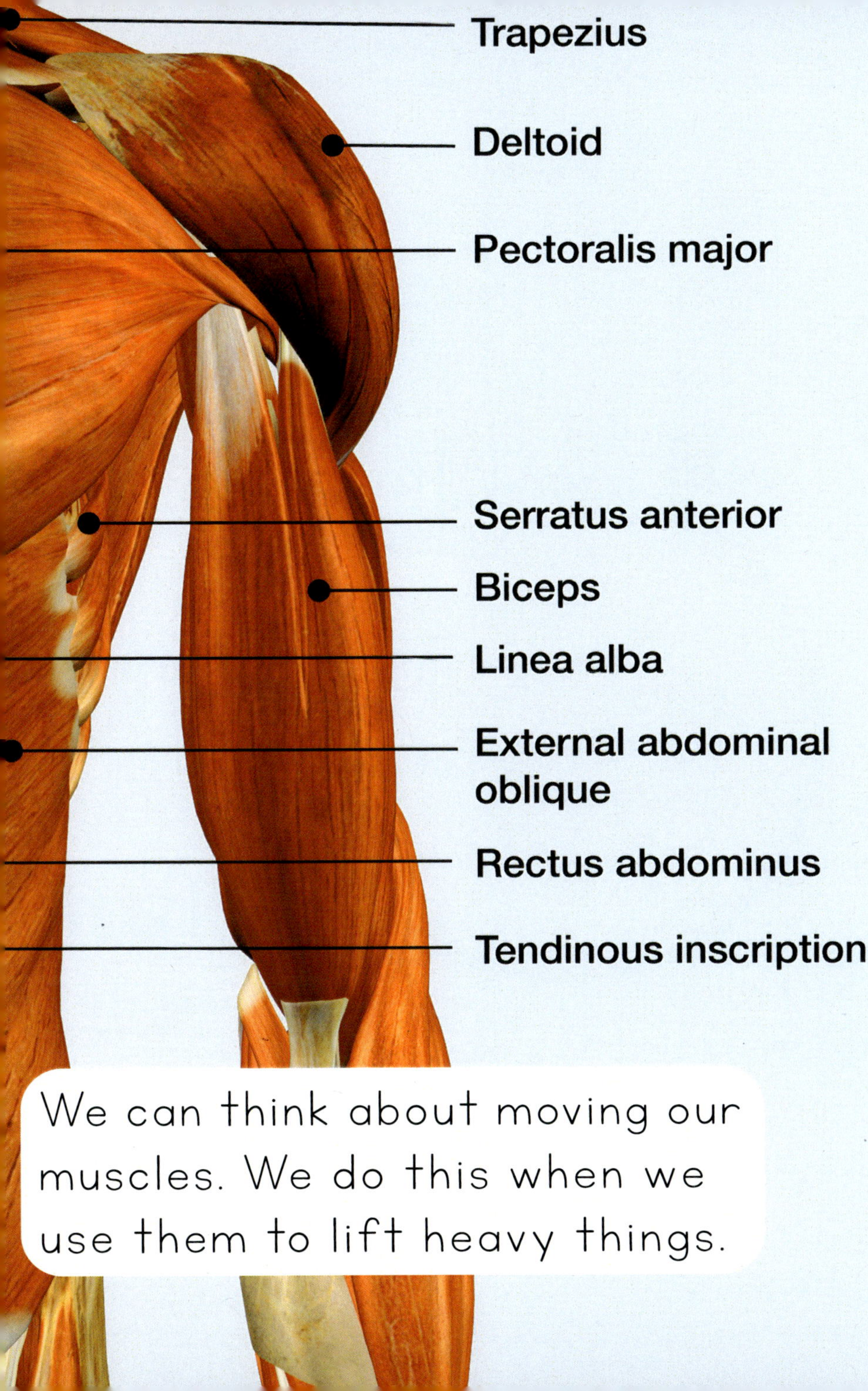

We can think about moving our muscles. We do this when we use them to lift heavy things.

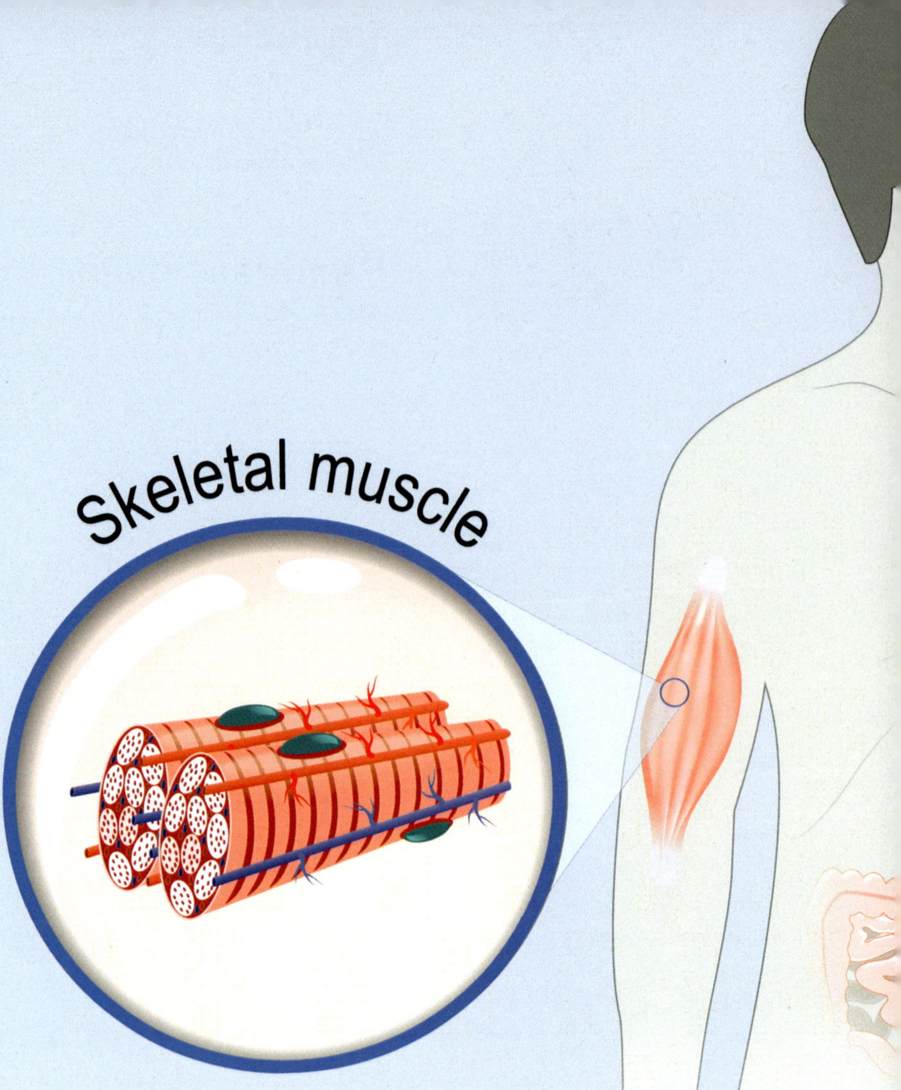

Some muscles work without us needing to think about them. Our brains or bodies tell them when they have to move.

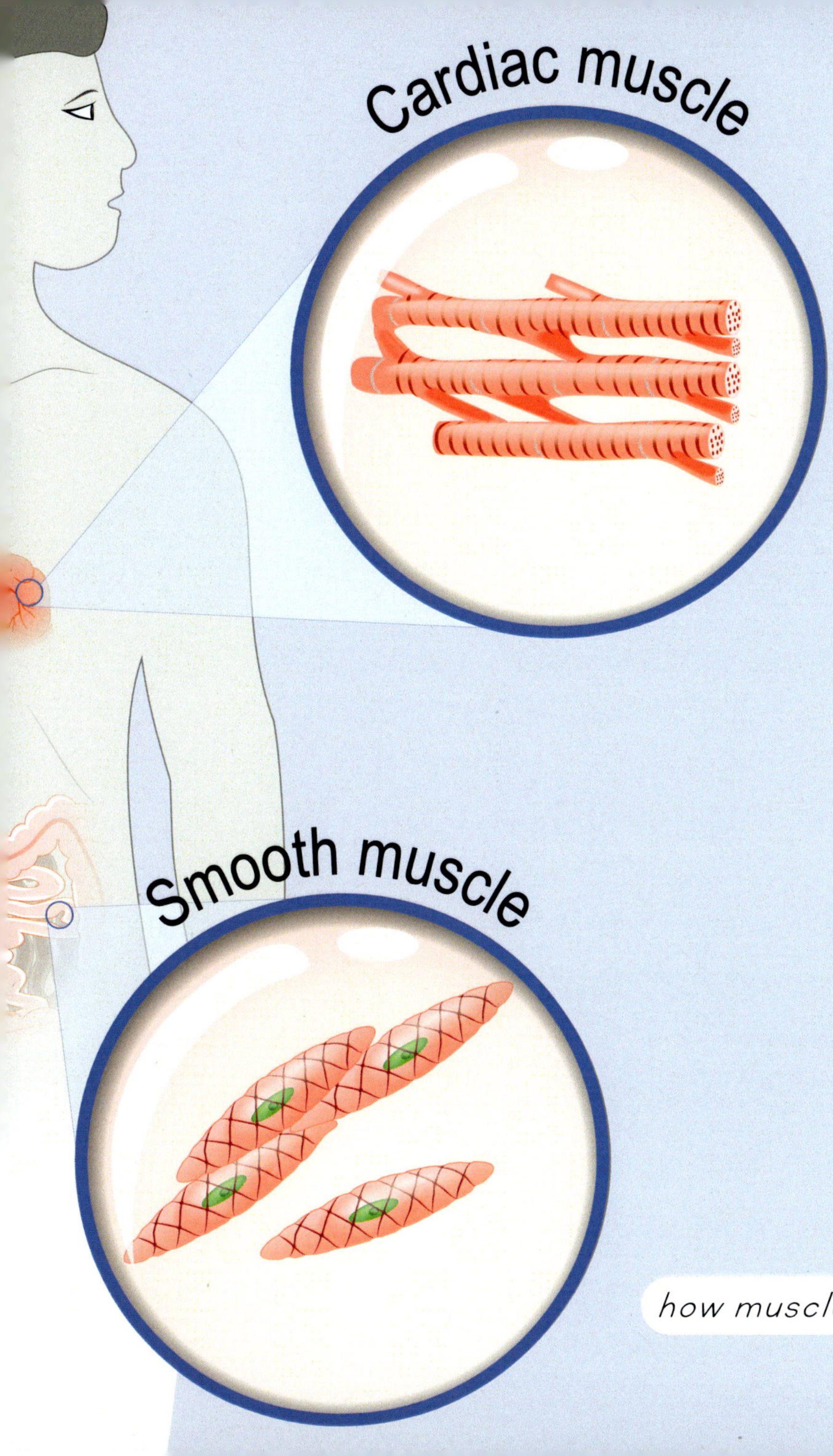
Cardiac muscle
Smooth muscle

Some muscles cover our bones and move our skeleton. These muscles give our body power.

skeletal muscles

Smooth muscles work the organs in our bodies. Our brain tells these muscles what to do without us even thinking about it.

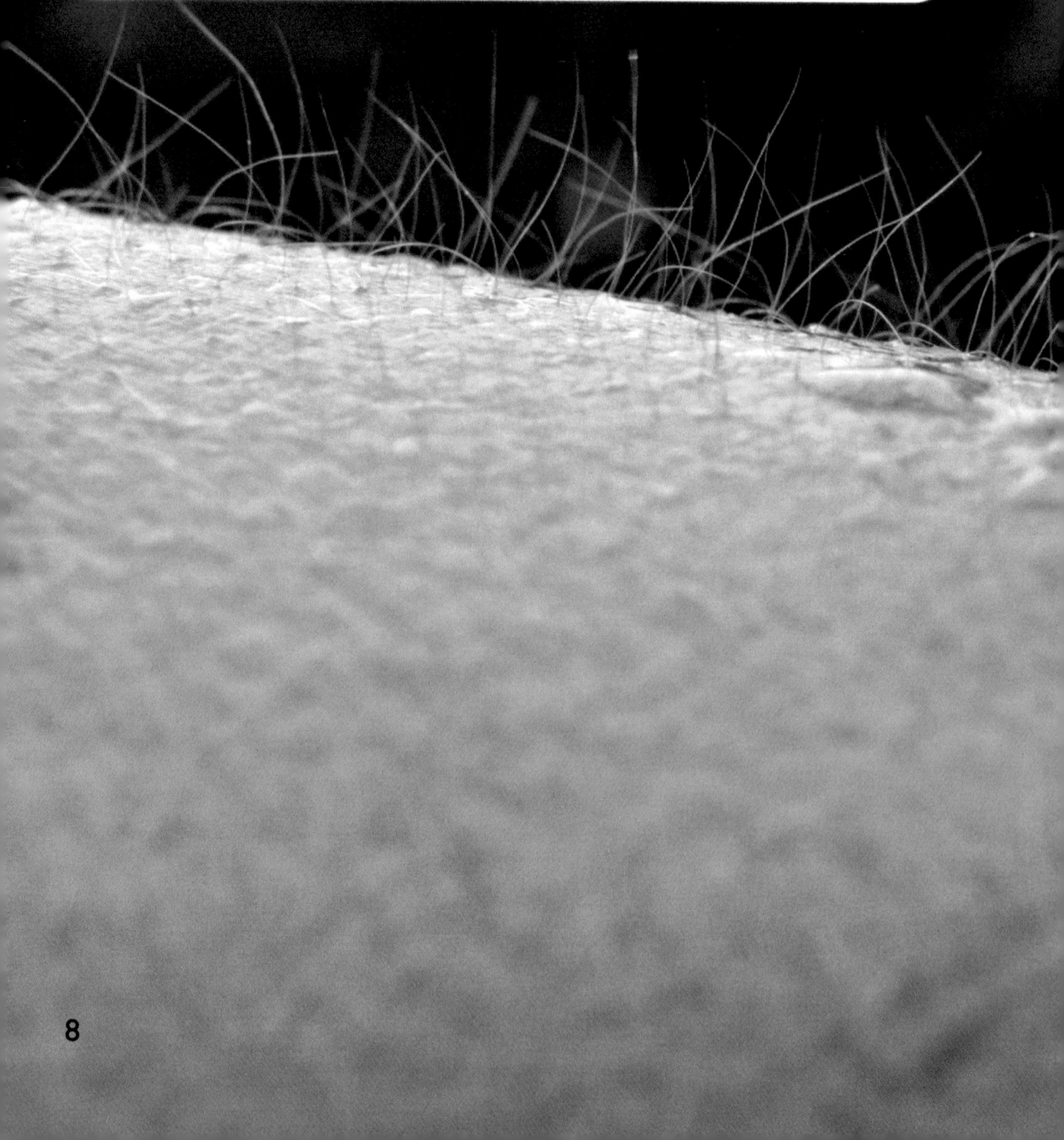

Smooth muscles help to push food through our body. They help our eyes to focus and make the hair on our bodies stand up when we are cold.

smooth muscles

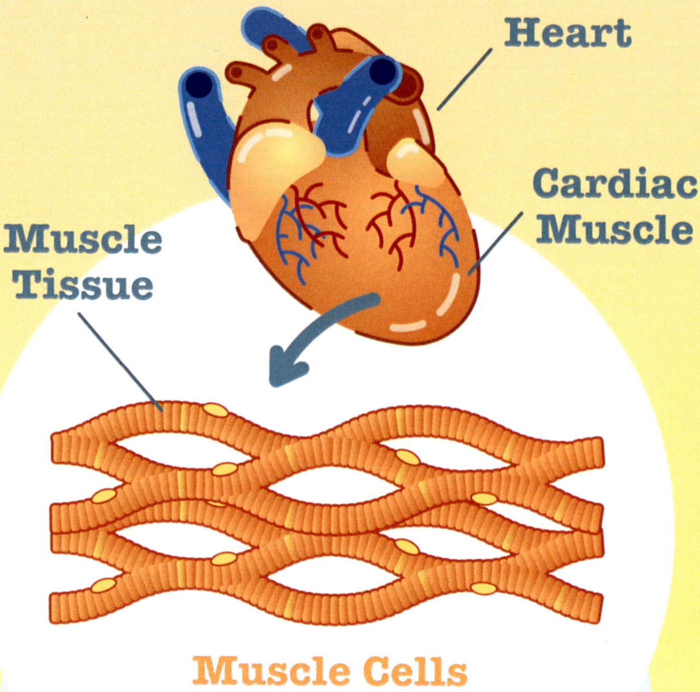

The cardiac muscle makes up the heart. Like a smooth muscle, it works without us thinking about it.

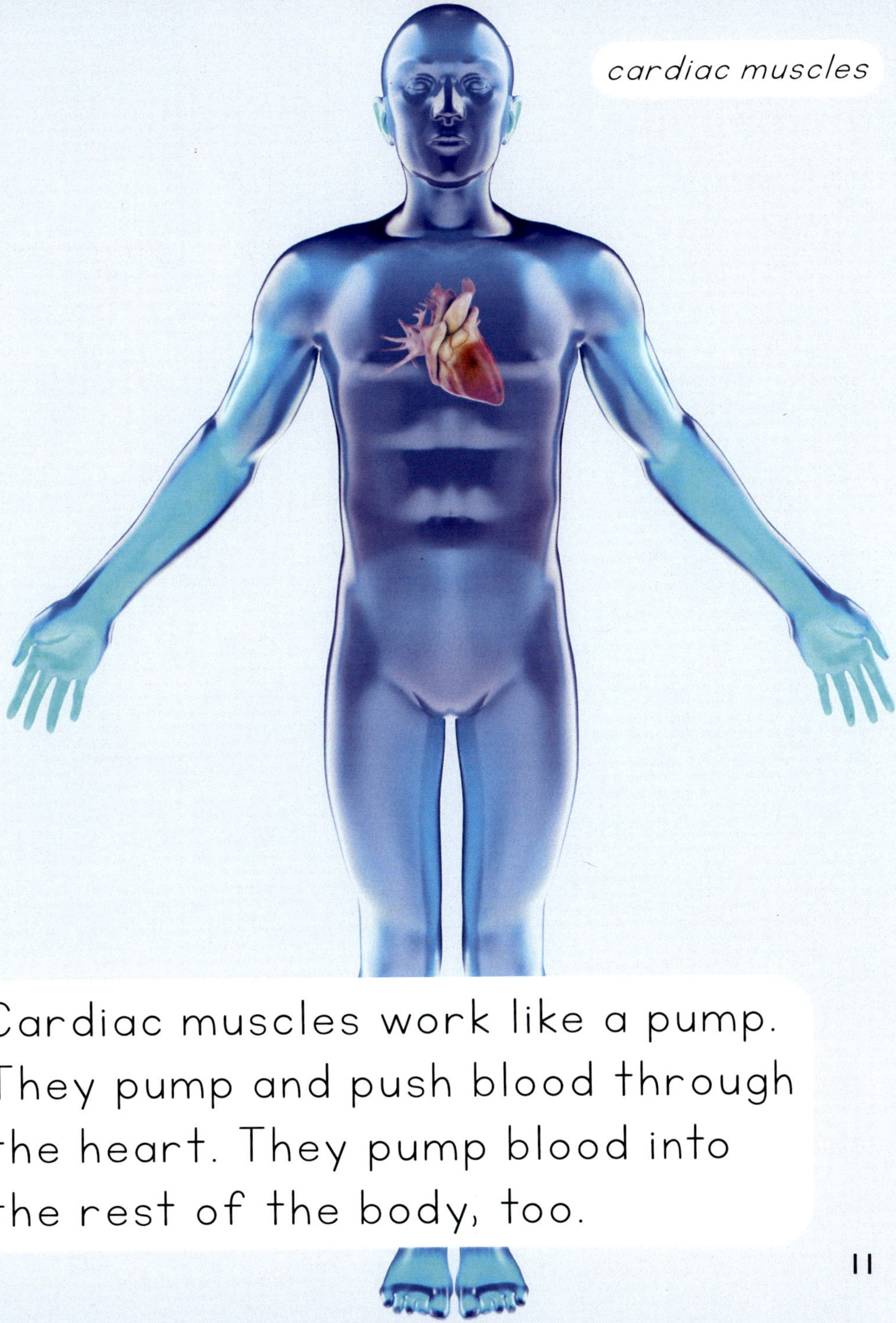

Cardiac muscles work like a pump. They pump and push blood through the heart. They pump blood into the rest of the body, too.

We have muscles in our face. Many of these muscles work with our skin to make our face do things.

facial muscles

Muscles need to move to keep them healthy. We can help them by making sure we exercise.

What we eat and drink can keep our muscles healthy. Vegetables, fruits, and grains will help to keep our bodies strong.

muscle memory

Our muscles know things if we do them many times. This is muscle memory. If we play a sport or music over and over, our muscles will know what to do.